WILLIAM TAYLOR

illustrated by Craig Smith

CHAPTER 1

No one ever found out where my dog, Harry Houdini, came from. All we knew was that he had escaped three times from death row down at the dog pound. That's how he got his name.

"Third time lucky, I guess," said Jack Rogers, the dog warden. "Can't think for the life of me why anyone would want to give the ugly mutt a home. This is what you owe me for pound fees." He handed Dad the bill.

"You've got to be joking, Jack," said Dad, taking out his wallet.

"I never joke," said Jack. "If you can get that mongrel to tell you how he got out of my pound, not once, but three times, just let me know. It's not going to happen again."

Jack Rogers told us that the first time Harry had escaped, he ended up in a flower shop. It had taken him and the florist two hours to corner Harry and drag him out. Harry wrecked every flower in that shop!

It was back to death row!

The second time he escaped, Harry made a bad mistake. I reckon Jack Rogers must starve the dogs in his pound because Harry made a beeline for the butcher's down the road. He wasn't hard to catch this time. The string of sausages Harry was dragging behind him got tangled around a lamp-post.

Old Harry wasn't going to let go of a good meal until it was all inside him. This took some doing because Harry had to unwind his dinner from the lamp-post and fight off two other hungry dogs at the same time. Harry and his sausages got their photograph in the paper.

Now, you might think it would be impossible to escape death row for a third time. There's no way out of *that* horrible place. "Well, there must have been a way," said Jack Rogers, "because the mongrel found it."

"Reckon he must have tied his sheets and blankets together and then gnawed through the bars on his window," said Dad to Jack. "Like you see in those old movies."

"It's not a joking matter," said Jack. "I don't give them sheets or blankets. Should've got the vet to put him down last night. No cheques. Cash only," he said to Dad.

If you think it was easy getting Mum to let me keep Harry Houdini, you'd be dead wrong. I begged for old Harry's life down on my bended knees. I promised to mow the lawns once a week for just about the rest of my life. I promised to wash the dishes every day and for ever and ever. I promised to wash the car!

Worst of all, I agreed to go without my pocket money for six months to pay for Harry's pound fees and his visit to the vet. Six months!

CHAPTER 2

"Good grief, Joe! What on earth is it?" asked Mrs Gribben, the local vet.

"It's my dog, Harry Houdini," I said, and I told her the whole story.

"You *sure* he's a dog? He's black. He's brown. He's grey and white. He's even a bit spotted in places!"

She looked closer. "Hmm. Short hair, long hair – some straight, some curly. Goodness gracious," she laughed, and she started on Harry's check-up.

"Come on, up you get," she said. Harry jumped up on the table. "Phew! Talk about bad breath," she said, holding a hand over her nose. "He stinks. Hmm, good strong teeth, though. Just need a bit of a clean."

"I'll buy him a toothbrush," I said.

"No need. I'll do it for him," said Mrs Gribben.

"What sort of dog do you think he is?" I asked.

"Well, let's see," she said. Harry grinned up at her. "Supposing that he *is* a dog ... front bit might be foxy. Could be a bit of spaniel ..." She peered closer. "Might even be a bit of sausage dog in there somewhere."

"Yeah. I know he likes sausages," I laughed.

"I couldn't even have a guess, Joe," she said, looking even harder.

"You've got to admit, though, he's not bad looking," I said.

The vet looked at me. "They say the customer's always right, Joe. Not this time, though. This is just about the ugliest dog I've ever seen – and I've seen a few in my time!"

"Take him home and put him in the bath – if your Mum is silly enough to let you – and shampoo him all over." She patted Harry. "Open wide, boy," she said and popped a couple of pills down his throat. "Worms," she muttered, and before Harry had time to breathe on her again, she gave him a couple of injections. "All things considered, you're not in bad condition, are you, Harry?"

"What about his teeth?" I asked.

"Bring him back next week, and I'll clean them," said Mrs Gribben.

"How much do I owe you?"

"Nothing, Joe. Anyone silly enough to give Harry a home is going to need every penny they've got."

"Gosh, thanks, Mrs Gribben," I said gratefully.

"Now," she smiled, "get him out of here before I change my mind."

CHAPTER 3

Harry Houdini took over our house. It was no good Mum saying that he had to live in our garage. It was no use Dad buying him a really long chain. Any dog clever enough to escape three times from death row at the dog pound is not going to have too much trouble living exactly where he wants to live!

Harry knew who had saved him. Harry was grateful. Harry was my dog. Harry was going to live with me! Not just around me, but right with me. He slept on my bed, in my bed, or under my bed – depending on his mood.

It took just one day for my room to start to stink like Harry, but I got used to it.

"Garage, Harry!" Mum would point. "Now!"

"Woof!" Harry would smile up at her and waddle off – for two minutes.

I'm certain that Harry could open doors. I am reasonably sure that Harry knew how to slither in through the crack under a closed door! I *saw* Harry climb in windows.

Dad put up a battle for a bit longer. "You keep that monster on the chain I got him, or I'll phone Jack Rogers," he thundered. "If you ask me, that dog deserves a fate *worse* than death!"

I was only half sure that Dad was joking, but saving Harry from "a fate worse than death" was a full-time job! On top of dish washing, car washing, lawn mowing, and general slavery, I now had to protect Harry.

Harry Houdini did not help matters. Harry Houdini did not understand that he needed protection. He did just about everything wrong. For one thing, he never stopped eating – I don't mean just dog sausage, dog junk, or nice juicy bones.

"Oh no-o-o-o," moaned Mum. "He's opened the fridge! He's eaten tonight's dinner ... and tomorrow night's! *And he's eaten a whole block of cheese!*"

Harry didn't stop at ordinary human food. Oh, no. In his first week as my dog, Harry Houdini ate the following non-human food:

1 cushion
2 shoes — not a whole pair, but one of Mum's and one of Dad's
Dad's best hammer (I think)
2 pot plants (and one was a cactus!)
Nearly four books (our Bible was a bit too big for Harry to finish)
Almost all of my sister Lizzie's second-best jersey
1 red plastic bucket.

"It's all right," said Mrs Gribben. "Harry's teeth are good and strong – and clean. He's munched it all up. It'll go straight through."

She was right. That red plastic bucket did go straight through! On top of all my other slave labours, it was my job to clean up all of Harry's messes. And he made messes non-stop – everywhere!

It was amazing just how small Harry Houdini's good, strong teeth had minced up that red plastic bucket. There were little piles of minced-up red plastic all around our garden, in the garage, and (I didn't tell Mum) right by my bed!

CHAPTER 4

"Why not take him to dog school," said Mum one morning. "It might help." She was taking some orange juice out of the fridge and padlocking it again. "It couldn't make him any worse, could it!"

"There's nothing wrong with Harry," I said.

"Nothing that a jab at the vet wouldn't fix," muttered Lizzie.

"Now, Liz," said Mum, "I won't have that sort of talk. I can't stand cruelty to animals."

"Wouldn't be cruelty," said Lizzie. "It'd be a kindness!"

"She's got a point," said Dad, pouring milk on his cereal. "Have you seen what's left of the lettuces I planted last week? All gone!"

"Yeah. You all blame Harry for everything, don't you?" I said. "Why would Harry want your lettuces, Dad? Could've been insects or moths or things."

"Never seen a moth that could dig such deep holes," said Dad.

"Bet there could be," I said as I slipped half a muffin to Harry. "In Africa, there could be."

"I'll phone June Morgan," said Mum. "I know she has something to do with training dogs. Now then, where have I put the key to the fridge?"

So Mum *did* call June Morgan, and Harry *did* go to dog school. (He lasted exactly twenty-three minutes before he got expelled.)

"Never met a dog that's beaten me yet," said Mrs Morgan to Mum and me at the beginning of the twenty-three minutes. "Sit, boy!"

"Get him off that dog!" yelled Mrs Morgan after three minutes. Harry was taking a ride round the dog-training ground sitting on top of a Great Dane. "Sit, boy!"

"Get him down from there!" yelled Mrs Morgan after seven minutes. Harry had climbed a tree. "Sit, boy!"

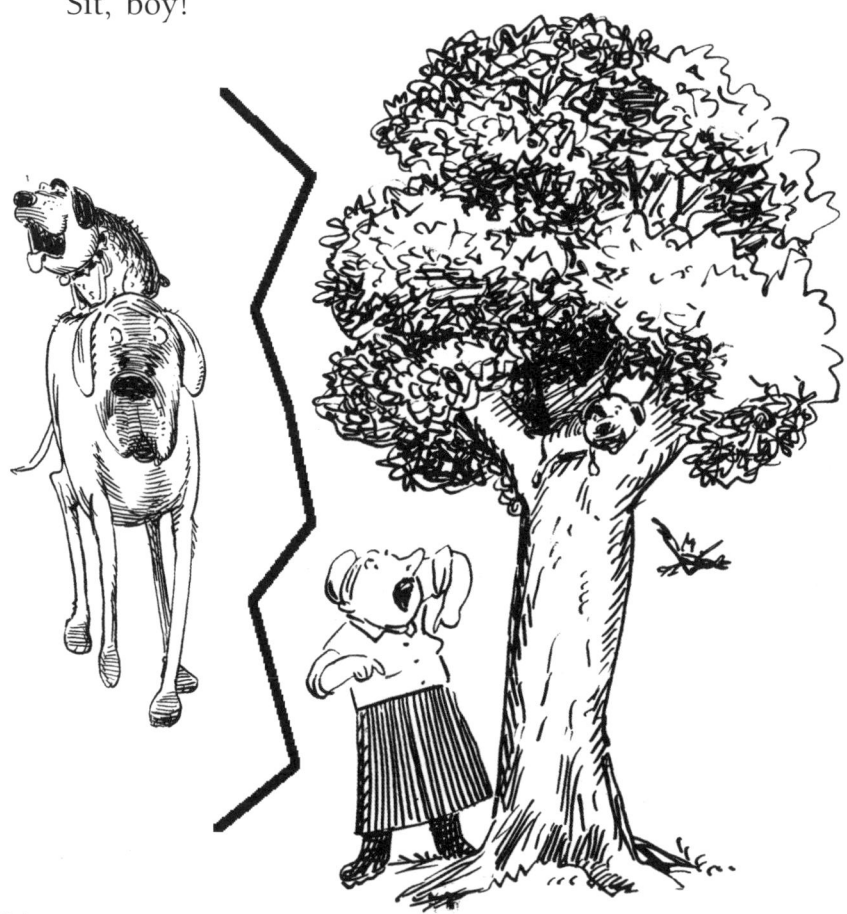

"Where on earth did he find that cat? Put it down!" yelled Mrs Morgan after nineteen minutes. "SIT, BOY!"

After twenty-one minutes, Mrs Morgan moaned, "Where are my headache pills? SIT, BOY!"

In the end, it was all too much. Harry was the dog that had beaten her. "OUT! OUT! OUT!" she screamed after twenty-three minutes. "A lifetime spent training pooches down the tube, down the drainpipe. Class is over!"

CHAPTER 5

After his session with Mrs Morgan, things were not looking good for Harry. But they got even worse, no thanks to Harry's poodle girlfriend, Fifi. Fifi lives with the Wrights at the end of our street, in a house with roses growing all over it.

Now, I'm not fussy when it comes to dogs, but if there's one dog that doesn't look *quite* like a dog, it's a poodle! And Fifi is as poodle as you can get – white, middle-sized, and trimmed like a hedge all over. Mrs Wright colours the fluff on Fifi's head pink and ties a ribbon in it.

This is how poor old Harry made things even worse for himself (and for just about everyone else). My sister Lizzie was going to be a bridesmaid for her best friend, Sharon. Sharon was going to marry Jim. But Lizzie nearly didn't get to be bridesmaid because Harry Houdini and Fifi ate her bridesmaid's dress. After Harry had dragged the dress outside and had a good gobble, Fifi wandered over for a nibble at the other half. Then Harry decided he wanted Fifi's half as well. Fifi didn't want to give it back. In the end, our garden was covered in little bits of Lizzie's dress.

It took all of Dad's strength and energy to stop Lizzie dragging Harry down to the vet.

"I'll fix *him*!" she shouted.

"No, leave it to me, Liz!" yelled Dad. "I'll take care of Harry!"

Fifi didn't look like a prize poodle any more. She was covered in dirt and mud. The ribbon had gone from her topknot, and apart from all the brown mud, she had little streaks of pink all down her face from her fancy hairdo. Mum tried to grab her to clean her up, but she ran through her legs. Poodles can be fast when they want to be.

It took all of Mum's strength and energy to calm Lizzie down. "Dry your eyes, girl. It's not the end of the world."

"It is. It is!" groaned Lizzie, the tears streaming down her face.

"We've got three days, Liz. I'm sure we can make you something else," said Mum.

It took all of Dad's *and* Mum's strength to keep Mr and Mrs Wright from attacking everything in sight. They were hopping mad.

Mr Wright – "With my bare hands! With my bare hands! Let me get at that dog!"

Round about then, I grabbed Harry Houdini and sneaked off and away.

Mrs Wright – "I'm laying a complaint with the authorities!"

Dad – "Lay an egg if you like!"

Mum – "Ross!"

Dad – "Sorry, Mrs Wright. Got carried away."

Mum – "Let's all go inside and have a cup of coffee … talk things over."

Mr Wright – "No!"

Mrs Wright – "Not today, thank you."

Dad (to me) – "Come back here with that mongrel dog! RIGHT NOW! This is the end, Joe. Now, come back here!"

CHAPTER 6

"We can't keep him, Joe," said Dad. "Harry's got to go."

"He's not that bad," I said.

"No," said Mum. "He's much worse!"

"I'll phone Mrs Gribben," said Dad.

"Why?" I asked.

"It's the only way, Joe," said Dad. "We'll have to have Harry put down."

"No!" I wailed. "Please, not that."

"Joe ..." Mum tried to hug me. I pushed her away.

"I love my dog," I sighed, and then I half gave in. "Couldn't we find Harry another good home?"

"Be reasonable, Joe," said Dad. "Who else would be mug enough to take him in, looking like he does?"

"It's not his looks that will put them off," said Mum. "It's how he behaves. You can't train him. Goodness knows, we've all tried."

"It's Lizzie's fault, anyway. All her fault. It was her stupid bridesmaid's stuff."

"It's no more Lizzie's fault than Mum's or mine," said Dad. "Harry has got to go. It'd be kinder to have him put down."

"Give me another week. Please? Let me try with Harry for just one more week?"

"You'll only make it harder for yourself, Joe. For all of us," said Mum.

"Just one week. Please?"

They sighed.

All this time, Harry Houdini lay quietly at my feet. His little brown eyes squinted up at me. He seemed to be saying, "Don't let them do it to me, Joe. I'll be very good. I promise."

As if!

"One week!" said Dad.

CHAPTER 7

You can't keep a good dog like Harry Houdini down for long. Not long at all. In the end, Harry saved himself. It must have taken some hard work and lots of dog brains, but Harry did it – he really did it!

Four days of what *might* have been Harry's last week on earth went by. He lived in the garage. He ate his dinners in the garage. He did all his business in the garage. Harry was as good a dog as Harry could be. He had no choice. He had two very strong dog chains to keep him there.

It was on a Saturday night that Harry became a hero. Lizzie was at Sharon and Jim's wedding. (Yes, Mum made another bridesmaid's dress for her!) Mum and Dad and I were over at Grandma's. Harry Houdini was the only one left at our house.

After we'd all left the house, two burglars smashed in our bathroom window, crawled into the house, and began stealing our stuff – TV, VCR, computer, Dad's whisky – anything that looked any good!

At exactly the same time, Lizzie and her boyfriend, Brett, had a stand-up fight at Sharon and Jim's wedding party. Lizzie left the wedding and walked home by herself.

Guess what? The burglars got more than they bargained for!

Now, I've only got Lizzie's word on what came next, but here it is.

Lizzie comes up the path, finds her key, goes inside the house, and gets grabbed by startled burglars.

"Help!" squeaks Lizzie and gets tape stuck over her mouth.

"Shuddup," say the burglars.

And then ... wait for it ... Harry Houdini saves his own life (and Lizzie's as well). Harry has *double unchained* himself, opened the garage door, taken one massive leap through the broken bathroom window, and, barking like crazy, has come to the rescue! The stunned burglars have never seen anything like Harry. They are scared witless.

"What the ...?" screams one.

"A werewolf!" screams the other.

Lizzie (so she says) gets her wits back and whacks one burglar out cold. Harry Houdini sinks his teeth into the other burglar and holds him down while Lizzie phones the police.

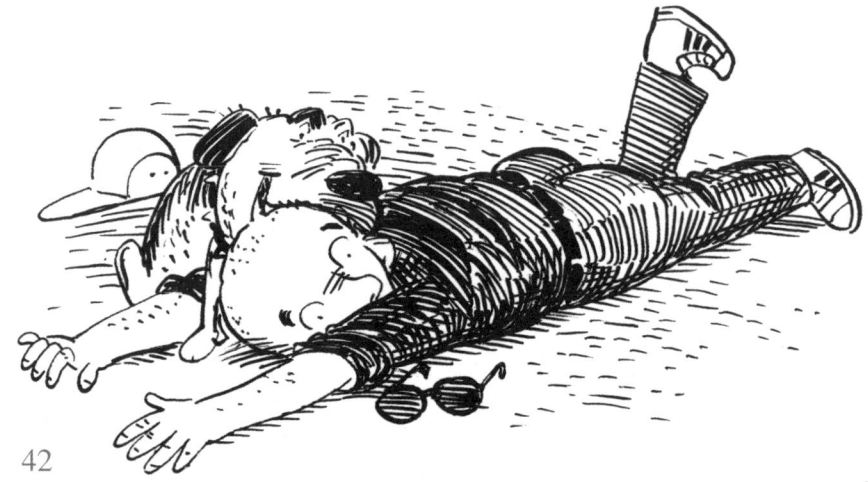

CHAPTER 8

Harry Houdini, *my dog*, is now a great hero, and all the good things in life have come his way. He's had his picture on the front page of our paper – for the second time!

"I don't want this old jersey any more, Harry," says Lizzie. "Have you got a use for it?" Has he ever!

"Never did like lettuce much," says Dad. "But you keep off those roses, Harry, or I'll skin you alive!"

"It's quite a good idea having a lock on the fridge," says Mum, looking at me. "If only I didn't keep losing the key. I think we'll all go out for pizza tonight. Yes, you too, Harry!"

Harry Houdini lives in my room all the time. My room still stinks, but at least Harry has started to do his business outside. He'll never have to go to the vet to be put down. But he does go for regular check-ups and to have his teeth cleaned – and all for free! "I still haven't decided whether you're a dog or not, Harry," Mrs Gribben says. "I've still got my doubts."

Well, I've got none.
Harry Houdini is all dog, and
Harry Houdini is my dog – well,
as much as any dog can belong to anyone! "Come on, Harry," I say, "let's go and do something." And sometimes we do just that – if Harry feels like it!

ARATA ISOZAKI
ACADEMY EDITIONS

THE ISLAND NATION AESTHETIC

Attempts have been made to locate sources of all photographs to obtain full reproduction rights, but in the very few instances where this process has failed to find the copyright holder, apologies are offered. Unless otherwise stated, all images are courtesy of the author: p8 Mitsumasa Fujitsuka; p11 (above left) and p22 (above left) Yoshio Takase, GA Photographers; p11 (below left) Shinkenchiku; pp16-17, p19 (all images), 20, 42-43 Yasuhiro Ishimoto; p22 (below left) Hisao Suzuki

First published in Great Britain in 1996 by
ACADEMY EDITIONS
An imprint of

ACADEMY GROUP LTD
42 Leinster Gardens, London W2 3AN
Member of the VCH Publishing Group

ISBN: 1 85490 437 X

Copyright © 1996 Academy Group Ltd. All rights reserved.
The entire contents of this publication are copyright
and cannot be published in any manner whatsoever
without written permission from the publishers.

Distributed to the trade in the USA by
NATIONAL BOOK NETWORK, INC
4720 Boston Way, Lanham, Maryland 20706

Printed and bound in the United Kingdom

CONTENTS

The Island Nation Aesthetic   6
1960 Blue Sky of Surrender Day: Space of Darkness   24
1965 Media, Illusion, Void: City Invisible   29
1970 Reduction to the Blank: Method, Manner   34
1975 Quotation and Metaphor: Work, Counter Architecture   39
1980 Style in Ruins: Time and Space = Time and History   46
Architecture With or Without Irony   53

THE ISLAND NATION AESTHETIC

■ In an essay written over one hundred years ago in 1891, entitled 'Intentions: The Decay of Lying', Oscar Wilde stated that 'Japan' or the idea of 'Japanese things' was purely an invention, an aesthetic fiction. According to him, there was no need to go to Tokyo in order to find 'Japanese things'; should the 'Japanese thing' not be found by studying the works of a certain Japanese artist in the comfort of one's home, thereby acquiring a Japanese style, and walking down Piccadilly with it, there would never be a hope of finding it.

The Japanese novelist, Natsume Soseki, a contemporary of Wilde, researched English Literature in London, after which he returned to Japan where he became the first creative novelist on the Japanese modern scene. Instead of writing about England *per se*, he elaborated a critical stance towards the complacent tendency of the Japanese modernisation that was then under way. And this, I believe, was thanks to his deep insight into 'England'. His England must have been very different from that of the English, but it must still have contained a glimpse of England's features.

Another contemporary of these two writers was Lafcadio Hearn, an Englishman known for his collections of Japanese folklore. While the narratives he collected in Japan were to some extent authentic, the kinds of images conjured up by his eyes and hands have now become 'Japan'. That is to say that the external gaze of the other, of the modern West, has been reconstructing Japan as a fiction. It is the nature of our time that we conceive Soseki's England and Hearn's Japan as solid pictures from which we can form our realities.

Following the teaching of Wilde, I once visited Lincoln's Inn Fields in London to write an essay on the Sir John Soane

Museum. The only reason I dared undertake such a wild scheme with my poor knowledge of English architecture was because I sensed a similarity between the English design and the design of the seventeenth-century Japanese architect, Kobori Enshu.

Enshu lived two centuries before Sir John Soane. One of the most representative examples of Japanese architecture, the Katsura Imperial Villa had long been attributed to Enshu, even by Bruno Taut. Today, it is commonly understood that the design was not by Enshu himself but by one of his followers. I have written an essay on the Katsura Imperial Villa, where I claim that the architecture which is now deemed legendary is in fact a text which allows multivalent interpretations, and that the style of the building consists of interpretation, selection and quotation from various early texts of Japan, China and even the West *(nanban)*. I sought to read into this textual manoeuvre a correspondence with my own manner of design for contemporary society (which I call *maniera*); and in the life of Sir John Soane, which was full of personal setbacks, and in his work, which always fluctuated between a rigorous system and complex images, I thought I saw an image similar to that I discovered at Katsura.

One day I noticed two books on these subjects sitting side by side on a bookshelf, and realised it is possible that two types of architecture from two different places (spatiality) and times (temporality) can be equidistant from my position, not to mention similar to my methodological preferences. One architecture was built in London one-and-a-half centuries ago and the other was built in Kyoto three-and-a-half centuries ago, but they are both, nevertheless, the same distance from me. Such a phenomenon tends to be ascribed to such terms as contemporaneity or textuality without history, and so on; however, what is of utmost importance for me working in Tokyo is that the Katsura Imperial Villa and the Sir John Soane Museum are spatially and temporally as far removed from me as possible. And it is this distance, a new distance, that is produced by the aesthetic fiction in the sense of Oscar Wilde. It should be stressed that despite being Japanese ourselves, today we see Japan with the eyes of a foreigner, precisely like those of Lafcadio Hearn or Bruno Taut. Indeed, having gone beyond the process of modernisation, we see Japan from a viewpoint similar to that of Westerners. It follows that the latter view of England incorporates the same mechanism of distancing as our view of England. There is of course the factor of geographical proximity, for instance, because of the easy access to Japanese things and places, I was able to enjoy the once-in-twenty-year opportunity to visit the hidden precinct of the Ise shrine, and I also know that the stone garden of Ryoan-ji Temple (although claimed to date from the fifteenth century) actually came to be arranged in its present form in the early nineteenth century. But notwithstanding this circumstantial benefit, I still see these Japanese things from the same distance as I do Stonehenge or the works of Sir Edwin Lutyens, for we all see these architectures as fictive constructs.

Tateyama Museum of Toyama, Youboh-kan Hall

For this reason, in order to design I determined to adopt an ambiguous stance by taking reality as an accumulated inheritance and reading it as fictive text. By a technique induced from a reading of text, the programme as given is disassembled and recomposed; this is the process I mentioned earlier as my manner (*maniera*). I will now explain how *maniera* produces ambiguity out of the parallel relations of reality/fiction and programme/text, using three of my current small-scale projects as examples. All of them were designed and constructed within the framework of the island nation. They all have peculiar, somewhat esoteric programmes, and my technique – drawn from my textual readings – might be quite idiosyncratic. However, there is a consistency, in that every project is the result of the pursuit of its own singular solution.

Ia
Youboh-kan
Tateyama Mandala
Modoki (mimicry)
Modoki (guise or mimicry) assumes a repetition of the original form. It can also be called simulation. Once a convention of ritual is composed, it becomes autonomous and everlasting through repetition.

Tateyama Mandala

Ib
Uji-an
Tea Ceremony
Toriawase (assortment)
In the tea ceremony, *Toriawase* (assortment) assumes the proper selection and arrangement of the implements and art objects which are utilised on each occasion; the objective is to make each ceremony unique. It might be thought of as an accumulation of quotations from the archives of beauty.

Ic
Nagi Museum of Contemporary Art
Picture of sun, moon, mountain and water
Mitate (diagnosis)
A picture of sun, moon, mountain and water, *Mitate* (diagnosis) is used to create a new articulation by expanding association through the analogy between Gestalts. It is, in a sense, an allusion. By drawing the transversal lines of 'family resemblance' between unrelated terms, *Mitate* marks the moment of naming.

Aesthetic products from Japan certainly possess specific qualities when compared with those from the West. However, forms and techniques seen in Japanese products were originally imported from the outside world – Korea, China and the West – rather than home-grown in Japan. What was first imported was then transformed into 'Japanese things' by the mechanisms of sophistication, adaptation, alteration and so on. I call this process 'Japanesque-isation'.

There seems to be a strange law governing this process. As one might notice, in Japanese history there has been a repetition of a particular chain of events: the movement from external pressure to civil war to importation to Japanesque-isation recurred in the seventh, twelfth, sixteenth and nineteenth centuries. These centuries mark the moments of heightened importation under external pressure and civil war, while the intervening years mark the periods of Japanesque-isation. Those aesthetic

FROM ABOVE, L TO R: 'Uji-an' teahouse; tea ceremony; Nagi Museum of Contemporary Art; picture of sun, moon, mountain and water

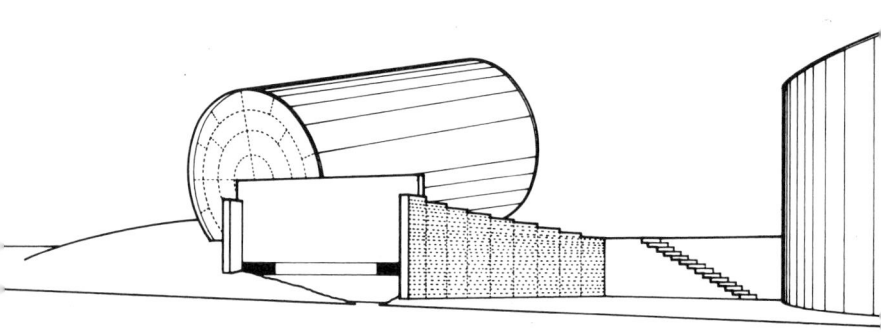

Arata Isozaki, Nagi Museum of Contemporary Art, perspective

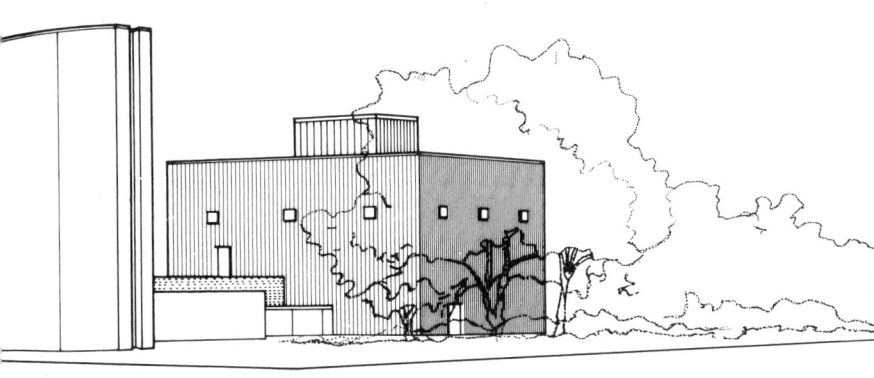

products which are considered to be 'Japanese things' always appear at the last phase of Japanesque-isation. Curiously enough, taking the appearance of the 'Japanese things' as a sign, Japanesque-isation always stops when a new external pressure bears down and leads into a new epoch, a new cycle. These are some examples of Japanesque-isation:

IIa
The Tale of Genji (eleventh century)
The technique of 'cloud and smoke' (*Un-en*), the technique of eliminating roof and ceiling in order to depict the narrative of the interior (*Fukinuki Yatai*)

IIb
The Stone Garden of Ryoan-ji Temple (fifteenth century)
The miniaturised landscape, microcosm

IIc
Hiroshige's *Fifty-Three Stages of the Tokaido*,
Sukiya Style building (eighteenth century)
Flattened perspective, transparency

IId
Walkman, headgear (twentieth century)
Lightness, popularisation

What causes the Japanesque-isation cycle to reoccur time and time again? One factor is the geopolitical condition of Japan as an island nation. In Japan, borders are invisible; what one sees instead is only the horizontal line of the ocean. In such a case as this, after the absorption of foreign pressure and the resolution of civil war, no sooner is the importation of foreign culture fully accomplished (as in a blood transfusion), than the nation immediately closes its ports. In the period of enclosure, hence, while its culture becomes more and more polished and refined, the social energy dries up. Accordingly, finally even

FROM ABOVE, L TO R: The Stone Garden of Ryoan-ji Temple; Sesshu's Ama-no hashidate; Hiroshige's Fifty-Three Stages of the Tokaido; Shugakuin-rikyu; Walkman; headgear

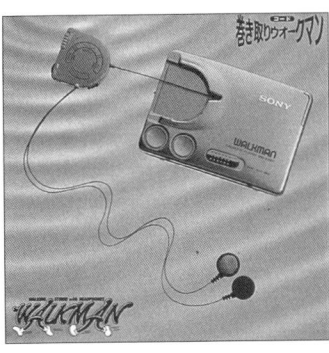

Arata Isozaki, Art Tower Mito, sculpture

aesthetic objects result in *wabi sabi*, the condensed and flattened sense of beauty. Such a condition – of an island nation – is ideal for producing something fragile and subtle.

To provide an example of an instance that motivates repetition, there is the ritualistic reconstruction of the Ise Shrine. In a ceremony that began in the seventh century, not only all the buildings of the shrine but also all the elaborate ceremonial implements were renewed, and the culmination came with the act of removing the God as a repetition/mimicry of the origami. This ritual of 1,300 years is motivated by an intense will to mimic the beginning.

IIIa
Ise, Ritualistic reconstruction

IIIb, c
Ise Japanesque = a creation of national style

In the notes to his collection of lectures on Hegel's *Phenomenology of Spirit*, Alexander Kojeve categorises Japan as a model of post-historical society. According to him, history in the Hegelian sense ended around 1600 in Japan, and for the past three centuries, people have lived a highly stylised life without war and forced labour. He called this Japanese way of life 'pure snobbery'.

I do not necessarily think that the 'end of history', as defined by Kojeve, precisely articulates the fate of Japanese society. Yet I have to agree that the aspect of life that follows certain formalised rules has long existed in Japan: for instance, society persists in the reconstruction of the Ise Shrine (as touched upon previously), in the tea ceremony and flower arrangement, and in lives wagered in Bushido, the Japanese ideal of chivalry. It seems that this element continues to survive in present-day Japan.

When the 'Japan Festival' took place in England several years ago, I worked as a commissioner for the exhibition, 'Vision of Japan', at the Victoria & Albert Museum. The theme of the

FROM ABOVE, L TO R: Ise Shrine; ritualistic reconstruction; Ise Shrine; Ise Shrine, Hottate-bashira

show I proposed was 'game'. I composed the whole exhibition in three sections: the past (*do* = way of discipline), the present (competition between corporations) and the future (virtual games). Games are based upon rules: from inside the game, its own derivation can never be questioned; by activating the rules to their limit, victory or defeat is dynamically challenged. The exhibition was intended to present how profoundly the game element permeates the Japanese convention of life and secondly, how this contributes to its technological, economic and aesthetic developments.

This is another aspect of the Japanesque-isation I mentioned earlier. I would like to stress once more the fact that Japanesque-isation is made possible by a closing of the ports, a possibility only for island nations. On an island something unique can be produced, free from any exterior disturbance. However, its aesthetic is born out of pushing the productive energy to the brink of death by drying out its living contingency. This might be an eroticism attained only by courting Thanatos to the most extreme proximity. I feel Oscar Wilde sensed this intuitively.

It can be said that Japanesque-isation has had a cycle of birth, death and rebirth, but this cycle now seems to be reaching the limit of acceleration. The process has paralleled a geopolitical transformation: the invisible border that existed only for island nations has come to be easily trespassed, and the nation-state at large has been losing its integrity. The

Team Disney Buiding

development of the information network and transformation of the modes of transportation have caused great confusion for many cultures by debasing the previously stable notion of borders. As a Japanese architect, I have been compelled to respond to this situation by determining my position: either to commit to reconstructing another framework for Japanesque-isation (as a nationalist) or working towards decomposing the framework (as a cosmopolitanist). This dichotomy that appears to be the only choice is, however, a false one. I believe I have to expand the peculiar sense of beauty and manner (*maniera*) my island nation has produced into the global dimension; to the extent, sometimes, that may even cause a conflict. I do this not only as a stranger to the West but also as a stranger to Japan. I will show you a few examples of such work.

IVa
Team Disney Building
Uji Byo-do-in
Cosmology
Cosmology is used as a guideline to determine the placement of the architecture. Representing the Buddhist Paradise in the Western direction (*Sukhavati*), the building rises like a phoenix on the opposite side of an artificial pond; in Florida, the arrangement of paradise is connected to the sun's course in heaven.

Uji Byo-do-in

FROM ABOVE, L TO R: Toyonokuni Libraries for Cultural Resources; Large Hall in Shoin style; Domus, La Casa del Hombre; Nageire-do

IVb
Toyonkuni Libraries for Cultural Resources
Large Hall in Shoin Style
Frame
Frame is a formalisation of *Chora* – becoming of a place. Used as a unit of such a nature, the cubic frame repeats itself into an infinite.

IVc
Domus, La Casa del Hombre
Nageire-do
Mask
The mask's function is to represent the face more strongly by hiding it than by revealing it as it is. In the same way as in *Noh* performance, the mask is used as a *maniera* to construct the facade of bewilderment.

Translated by Sabu Kohso

1960 BLUE SKY OF SURRENDER DAY: SPACE OF DARKNESS

■ The sky over the archipelago was a cloudless blue on August 15, 1945, the day Japan surrendered. At that time I was a boy in my mid-teens and although I sensed that an era was ending, I had no idea what was beginning. All I knew was that the roaring had stopped and, for an instant, there was unmitigated calm.

Now, as I look at a photograph of a Vietnamese Buddhist priest committing self-immolation, I recall the flames of the countless foreign-made automobiles which had been overturned and set alight in front of Tokyo's Imperial Palace in 1952 on what is now called Bloody May Day. Similar flames had set ablaze the skies over Japanese cities after B29s had scattered their incendiary bombs – known as Molotov bread baskets. These had little restraining influence on me, as, in spite of the war, I continued to play in childish innocence.

Throughout my youth, until I began to study architecture, I was constantly confronted with the destruction and elimination of the physical objects that surrounded me. Japanese cities went up in flames. Forms that had been there an instant earlier vanished in the next.

The ruins that formed my childhood environment were produced by acts of sudden destruction, unlike those of Greece and Egypt which had long been in a ruinous state. Wandering among them instilled in me an awareness of the phenomenon of obliteration, rather than a sense of the transience of things.

On the day in 1960 when the Japanese-American Security Treaty was ratified, I was a member of a protest demonstration in front of the Prime Minister's official residence. An abandoned armoured car had been parked sideways across a narrow sloping street beside the residence and a group that seemed to be right-wing had occupied it. They probably thought this side street, which was blocked, would be an excellent place to trap and thrash any of the protesting students and citizens milling around the Diet building. I was part of a barricade intended to isolate the armoured car. As it grew late and we all began to feel tired, both groups mingled and joked with each other until it was impossible to tell friend from foe.

For about a week I had patrolled the Diet building and by the time the ratification took place, late at night, I was very weary. In previous demonstrations I had been obsessed with the fantasy of seeing the Diet building, which looks like a preposterously large gravestone, set alight like the buildings which I had seen during the war. Although a female student, who tried to crash into the Diet, was killed, there was no fire. The tension in our group began to crumble that night. I happened to catch a glimpse of the eyes of a man, who all night, virtually without moving, had stood in a position of leadership on top of the armoured car, waiting for a signal. He and his group must have experienced a despair more dreadful than ours.

After the struggle over the treaty was finished, the two things that remained in my memory in connection with it were the Diet building, which did not go up in flames after all, and the eyes of the man who, then, at any rate, was my enemy.

At about this time a group of my artist friends began behaving in eccentric ways on busy street corners. Calling themselves the Neo-Dadaist Organisers, they rashly opposed everything connected with existing institutions, organisations and systems. I sympathised with their belief that only destructive behaviour can be called art and sometimes participated in their activities. At one point, Shusaku Arakawa, a member of the group, and

I proposed planning a house that would be impossible to live in – of course the plan was never realised.

In 1960, the Metabolist Group was formed and began designing cities of the future. The members of the group were friends, all about my age. Whereas they were all independent architects attempting to establish their own methodologies, I was still employed in the offices of Kenzo Tange and URTEC, where I was in charge of the 'Tokyo Plan', a scheme for a futuristic city stretching its backbone over the waters of Tokyo Bay. The spare time I had after work was spent engaged in political demonstrations and the anti-productive debauchery of artists' groups, leaving me very little freedom for planning on my own.

The thinking behind Japanese architecture in the fifties had been to attempt to unify traditional Japanese wooden structures with Modernist architectural space, in which interior and exterior could interpenetrate. It could be termed a Japanese version of the New Empiricism and New Brutalism popular in Europe at the time. The Metabolists proposed bold technical innovations and, by means of their proposals for cities of the future, attempted to break the current architectural thinking. In the sixties Japan experienced miraculous economic growth, consequently cities were rebuilt and expanded. Metabolism's ideas and methods accurately reflected prevailing circumstances, making it the leading architectural ideology of the time.

Metabolist architecture celebrated the industrial society. These architects believed that architecture was a durable consumer item. Consequently, their use of exterior capsules, units and panels was not necessarily a solution founded in theory but lauded the industrial society by displaying mass-produced elements and indicating the ways in which they could be replaced and altered.

I was dissatisfied with politics, art and my own field of architecture in 1960, but unable to break through with a methodology of my own, I became frustrated and day after day spent my energy on physical participation in radical activities.

At about that time I was given a chance to publish a project entitled 'Incubation Process' in an art magazine. In this context I abandoned all the technical considerations with which, as an architect and planner, I had been compelled to deal, and concentrated solely on the materialisation of a concept that was then in the process of genesis.

The result was a single photomontage which was extremely illogical and therefore neither architecture, poetry, urban planning, philosophy, a picture, a comic, nor a diagram. This photomontage liberated me from psychological suppression. By cutting ties with the architect's methods, the rational support of which is technology, I felt that I was once again able to strive to be an architect. Forced into a corner and almost desperate, I had discovered a breakthrough.

Later, this photograph was frequently cited as a representative Metabolist work. But while I was certainly thinking in Metabolist terms in this montage, as I dealt with the flux of generation and the destruction of the city, I was never a member of the Metabolist group. Indeed, I always tried to make a clear distinction between myself and their technological orientation, their somewhat naive pragmatism which allowed them to believe that a social revolution could be achieved by means of new technology.

My next task was to define the image of the kind of architect I wanted to be. The following passage, from some of my notes written in about 1960, has a bearing on this image:

> In my opinion, the minimum requirement of an architect is a concept that germinates within himself. Though it may correspond organically to reason, design and all the phenomena of actuality and non-actuality, this concept must exist without connection with any of these things. The existence of the concept can be proven only when the concept itself can be conveyed to others. It probably becomes certain and unshakeable in accordance with the nature of the medium through which it is conveyed; I want to discover the medium that will make possible its

most accurate transmission . . . In the search, architectural design is my professional means.

To discover the concept, I sought ideas for the interpretation of space, time and matter (architecture and cities), all three solely as metaphors. My equations for them are space = darkness, time = termination (eschatology), and matter, or architecture and cities = ruin and ashes. I have written essays on all three topics: 'Space of Darkness', 'Process Planning' and 'City Invisible'. Darkness, termination and ruin are incapable of being given form, they are diametrically opposed to such socially recognised concepts as transparency, progress and construction, and have an aura of the unfortunate about them. Although I considered a paradoxical stance using these concepts as an effective means of countering architecture as it existed at the time when technology reigned supreme, no one in the Japanese architectural world took me seriously.

Oddly enough, these metaphorical images relate to my memory of that instance of total tranquillity, when everything seemed to have stopped, that I experienced on the day of the Japanese surrender. The destruction of houses and buildings that we had considered mainstays of our way of life; the established belief of the national state with the Emperor at its head; and the social system that controlled even the smallest daily activities, had collapsed and vanished, leaving behind only the void of the blue sky overhead.

Infinite darkness lies behind the blue sky. The stopping of time is a termination like the eschatological interpretation of the end of the world. The burned-out cities which I saw before me were ruins. Perhaps subconsciously I am attempting to return to that remembered instant which changed history and to conceptualise that moment in the form of architecture.

1965 MEDIA, ILLUSION, VOID: CITY INVISIBLE

■ It is perfectly acceptable to consider cities as a flux of generation and destruction but, in doing so, the nature of time must be examined. Having learned the ideas of mobility and change from Team X, the Metabolist architects attempted to think of architecture and cities in terms of the Buddhist idea of transmigration. They made no general observations, instead they proposed the concrete mechanism of architectural composition: a more or less permanent framework with changeable elements plugged into it and a smooth order governing the relations between the two. As the name of the movement reveals, they took the metabolism of organic creatures as the model of the kind of change they posited. Without delving into the philosophy of time, they were more concerned with the foreseen harmony of alteration systematically taking place within the flow of the time in which transmigration takes place.

I was in agreement with most of what they said but could not see eye to eye on one cardinal point: drawing a direct analogy between organic metabolism and architectural composition. For rather than being systematic, change is dramatic and destructive, lying outside the bonds of human control. It is the result of complicated accumulations of overlapping, unforeseeable coincidences. Method and logic originate on the basis of a toleration of the natural course of change.

Since change is half-destructive and half-constructive, it should be permissible for architecture to create the exact appearance of ruins.

When Tokyo was rebuilt after World War II, it accommodated examples of the weird generation of accumulated coincidences. The cheap room which I rented as a college student was located in one of these disorderly places. The wooden building, a capricious conglomeration of repeated additions located on a gently sloping bank, was devoid of the systematic placement, lucidity and order that are generally recognised as the characteristics of traditional Japanese residential architecture. To reach my room, which was in the innermost part of the building, one walked up two or three steps and down a diagonal corridor, then up a flight of stairs that turned twice along the way, then down a corridor leading to the left and up still another flight of steps. The side of the bank was covered with an irregular mass consisting of a small part of the original building plus a number of additions necessitated over the years by dismantling and alterations of function and repairs.

In later years I tried referring to it as a topological labyrinth, but actually the neighbourhood was a slum. Before the war it was a rundown region for poor labourers, now it was a sunless ravine and bank on which my boarding house was located. Small houses crowded in on each other, and no doubt the cats that wandered from roof to roof had a better idea of the overall space than the human inhabitants.

My boarding house was not level and plumb: the books that I arranged along one wall were so heavy that my room gradually tilted in one direction. From time to time, the landlord would prop it up. My first priority was to move, but before I did I became interested in the entire region and its complicated spaces: the disjointed spatial connections; the spontaneous happenings; the capricious appearance and disappearance of spaces; the conjunctions of multifarious and diverse functions; the many layered spaces; the corridors that twisted like a Möbius strip; doors that produced both awful noises and beautiful voices; and people living together with rats, ticks, goldfish and grasshoppers.

Ruins clearly reveal themselves in the process of construction and alteration. In the War many Japanese cities lost all their old forms, but they were rapidly filled with groups of buildings that, from the very outset, looked like ruins with no visual order. Steel and concrete mixed with advertisements, neon lights and telegraph poles came in and passed out of existence easily. Cities lost their monumentality behind an aggregation of flickering, lightweight and superficial elements. They began to convey their meanings to us through semiotic codes rather than actual solid forms. The development of various kinds of new media intensified this trend.

The city is undeniably in a state of flux. Invisible, it is virtually simulated by the codes that fill it. In my 'Invisible City', which alludes to ruins, I foresaw a city filled with unreal codes where the interpretation of the classical structure of cognition is meaningless. I now believe that design and city planning will become impossible using methods which involve only the manipulation of physical actualities. Since coming to this conclusion, although I regard cities as fit objects for consideration, I have ceased to think that they can be designed and hence, no longer undertake work of that kind.

In thinking about architecture, more than the city, time reveals itself in naked form. Designing a building, of course, means making visible something which has never before existed. The time involved in composing a piece of architecture is absolute and essentially different from time as expressed in the change and metamorphosis of the Metabolist architects. In 'Process Planning', I interpret time in architecture from a completely different viewpoint. The idea of 'growing architecture', which was popular when I wrote the article, is the reverse of the process that produces ruins.

In the normal process of creating architecture, at the final minute it is necessary to freeze all alteration. In the search for that moment of freedom, I made use of the ancient Judaic eschatological principle that the world must someday come to an end. Imagining the ultimate end is a dynamic viewpoint, clarifying the direction in which present conditions flow. On the drawing board, the piece of architecture is allowed to grow and change until it reaches its ultimate point in time, its termination, then it is cut off at the juncture called the present. It is then fixed and leaves the architect's hands. It may change thereafter, but it is meaningless to try, as the Metabolists did, to foresee its future alterations. It is not for the architect to speak of its future.

In this connection, the time that exists in the architect's concept emerges. This is different from absolute time, which flows unbroken from the past to the future.

In explaining the moment of enlightenment, the great Buddhist priest Dögen (1200-53), who was the first person to give Zen teachings a firm systematic foundation in Japan, wrote of flying towards a given instant. However, the same notion of time has existed in the Orient since the distant past. For instance, in the *Abhidharma-kosha-shastra* by the fifth-century Buddhist priest and scholar Vasubandhu, there occurs a clear definition of time as a single moment. Everything before the emergence of a *dharma* (entity) is the past and everything after its disappearance is the future. The moment before the eyes is the present. In this version, time is included within the entity.

In my architectural method I combine the dynamism of the Judaic idea of termination and the Buddhist concept of time as reduced to the instant. The final section of 'Process Planning' sets forth the way in which architecture that has grown in reverse from the terminal minute is frozen in an instant. In other words, the building ceases to progress towards growth and instead begins moving in the direction of ruin. For this reason, my doctrine lacks the optimism derived from the future of eschatological thought and is closer to the Buddhist doctrine of the impermanence of all things.

Many of the ideas that went into the formulation of this viewpoint were developed during work on a joint research project that resulted in a volume called *Niho no toshi kükan* (Japanese Urban Space). This study revealed that many of the characteristics of Japanese cities cannot be adequately explained on the basis of Western urban concepts. Our study was a method of analysing those elements.

The traditional Japanese city consisted of buildings made largely of wood, paper and straw, which could easily be turned to ashes, and did not readily reveal itself to the eye. It was governed by a vague awareness of the mood of a busy neighbourhood (*kaiwai*). I have come to think that the old-fashioned neighbourhood feeling is becoming a characteristic of the modern Japanese city too.

Work on this project resulted in 'Invisible City' and led to the development of the idea of 'Darkness' as an architectural prototype.

Counterpoising invisibility and darkness with highly visible and substantial cities and architecture made my methodology more conceptual and metaphorical. Architectural design is the process of giving concrete form to intangible concepts. In this process it is first necessary to pick out all the things that denote architectural elements; then it is necessary to create a mechanism that will give new meaning to these now neutralised elements. This is the starting point of my architecture.

1970 REDUCTION TO THE BLANK: METHOD, MANNER

■ In some respects, the year 1968 may be compared with the year 1527, when papal Rome was sacked, occupied and pillaged by the Spanish. Although the occupation was only temporary and the papal authority was restored with the passage of time, this incident destroyed Rome's character as a cultural centre and gave birth to the possibility of Mannerism.

In 1968, the Chinese Cultural Revolution ignited sparks all over the world that fired students and other young people to acts of demonstration. Schools, offices and galleries were occupied, and liberated zones were set up in many great cities. Although strategic and important areas were targeted, most of these uprisings were spontaneous attempts to overthrow the authority of the Establishment and transcend the usual boundaries between right and left, or conservative and revolutionary.

I was pleased to observe this explosion of anarchic energy since I viewed it as agreeing with my own self-imposed programme for the overthrow of architectural Modernism. Some years earlier, I had designed the Oita Prefectural Library, which was made with unfinished concrete – 'béton brut'. This building was the Japanese realisation of the New Brutalism, and I was, in effect, signifying my graduation from all the things I had learned from Modernism up to that point. The next task was the dissolution of Modernism.

Ridding myself of a Modernism that pervaded my whole being was difficult. It was a tautological paradox to attempt to employ Modernist vocabulary, the only vocabulary I could use, in dismembering Modernism. Such was my dilemma in 1968.

In the month of May, that same year, I was put in charge of a corner at the fourteenth Milan Triennial. My project, which was called 'Electric Labyrinth', used light, projections, sound and music to involve the visitor in a technologically created environment. In the display, ghost-figures from the Edo period of Japanese history (1600-1867) overlapped with the ruins of Hiroshima and the destruction of the city of the future in what amounted to a criticism of modern urban planning for doing no more than painting rosy, Utopian pictures. From the day of the opening ceremonies, however, my space was occupied by someone else. In the hall were a few other works reflecting ideas similar to my own, but no matter what the ideas, everything had to fit into the established Triennial pattern. This may be why my place was taken from me. From the outset, this exhibition was intended to celebrate and circulate products of the industrial society. It is self-contradictory to attempt to criticise modern design through Modernism. I repeatedly asked myself whether the only way to shake the system was to resort to violent contestation.

At the same time, I found myself in a very difficult situation in connection with the World Exposition held in Osaka in 1970 (Expo 70). As a representative of Kenzo Tange, who was the general producer, I participated in the design from the outset and was personally responsible for designing the equipment for Festival Plaza – the central facility of the entire exposition. In addition, I was technical producer for the opening-day ceremonies. A national event like a world exposition is naturally an important target for debate, and I was criticised for taking part in it. Whilst emotionally sympathetic to my critics, whose views I understood, I nevertheless had a professional architect's responsibility to complete work that had long been contracted:

At one time, brilliantly coloured spaces began to fade,

the shadows began to disappear from objects with definite outlines, and the sense of their existence began to grow vague.

I cannot say precisely when I started to see things in this way, although I suspect it was probably while making preparations for Expo 70, which always reminded me of a space in which a box of toys had been overturned.

At the time, I acted like the headmaster in those preparations: making proposals, drawing-up working plans, taking part in the activities of site-control groups, and advocating colour-scheme diversity. Then, when everything was as I wished, it was impossible for me to cry out that everything was wrong – but it *was* wrong. I could tell that something invisible and indefinite was missing behind the displays, the organisation, the shows, the crowds and the information media. I witnessed the process from which this deficiency came.

I was overcome with tremendous fatigue. When this happened, images that had formerly presented themselves to me in bright colours, faded like overexposed photographs, leaving nothing but tones of sepia and white.

Fatigue was not the whole problem. I was completely, physically rundown. I collapsed one morning and had to leave the Expo grounds in a wheelchair which was loaded on a Boeing 727 with a forklift. It happened on the very day when the Emperor and the Crown Prince visited the Expo grounds and when the robots I had designed danced to the *Kimi ga yo* (the Japanese national anthem), as flower petals rained down from the great roof covering the Festival Plaza.

For months I lay idle in bed, once again the victim of a psychosomatic crisis which visits me at intervals of about a decade. This was the gravest seizure I had yet experienced. The first time I had been stricken, ten years earlier, fatigue had been the cause. I now concluded I had to leave the Kenzo Tange office and set up on my own. Confronting hospital gloom, I resolved then to make darkness and ruin the basis of my theories of space and time.

I had found myself in the embarrassing position of being a critic of Modernism who was taking a professional part in Expo 70, a national event in which the Modernist vocabulary was the only one permitted. This predicament created great nervous tension and ruined me physically.

Under these circumstances, colours faded for me and I began to see only blanks. Substances lost mass and became only shadows. I felt as if the twilight instant, known as the devil's hour, had settled on the whole world. I resolved that when I designed buildings from that time forward I would strive to pursue the blank as far as possible; return physical objects to a colourless state; and formulate the way I did this into a methodology.

Making multi-dimensional spaces from concrete objects necessitates basic lines and compositional units to serve as minimal clues. Though they were my ultimate concepts, from the standpoint of physical architecture, blankness and twilight can be nothing but metaphors achieved by means of neutralised geometry and meticulously controlled conditions of lightbeam distribution. The device which I ultimately hit on was the use of a grid composed of homogenous, limitless, square compartments to cover exterior surfaces. My entire visible world was to be covered with this grid of equal squares.

The trap inherent in this situation is the impossibility of covering surfaces with anything other than points of minimal units. This is where geometrical figures must come into play.

It is essential to seek forms that have been reduced to their minimum, since they are the only ones that can be used in actualising blanks. The square is abstracted from the equally divided grid. At the same time, the circle, which encompasses unit surface with the minimum possible outline, comes to mind. Applied multi-dimensionally in architecture, the square and circle generate the cube, the cylinder, the sphere and the regular tetrahedron; composed of right-angles and enclosing a minimum volume with equal sides. From ancient times, these naturally evolved, basic forms have been called the Platonic solids.

At the time of my second crisis, I had arrived at the point

where I was determined to reorganise and reduce all my architecture to the forms of the Platonic solids. During this reorganisation, the tide of protest which heralded a season of political reform, suddenly ebbed. However, Modernist architecture had clearly completed its union with the authorities in control.

In 1527, the sack of Rome by the Spanish destroyed its importance as a cultural centre. In my view, in 1968, the collapse of both seamy-side functionalism and the Modernist concept of progress toward Utopia through the leadership of the avantgarde served as a boundary. Thereafter, Modernism in architecture lost its social effectiveness.

Reduction to the blank and attachment to the Platonic solids constituted my criticism of Modernist architecture. A tendency toward formalism was my political choice for the seventies, and I organised it into the doctrine which I describe as *maniera*.

1975 QUOTATION AND METAPHOR: WORK, COUNTER ARCHITECTURE

■ As I have shown, the age of contestations demanded fundamental tautological paradoxes in the intellectual realm. It contained the self-contradiction inherent in a situation when, because the production of a different tool is impossible, it is essential to use a system's vocabulary to criticise the system itself. I had studied Modernist architecture, and its production methods were part and parcel of me. I was confronted with the virtually unsolvable problems of discovering a way to effect the dissolution of the visible and invisible vocabulary, involving it intimately in the whole of society. As long as I was limited to the Modernist vocabulary to attain this goal, I could do nothing but go around in circles.

It may be possible to employ violence to bring about the collapse of a social system, but that collapse cannot be truly fundamental as long as the logic of the vocabulary of the social system is used in its destruction. In such circumstances, things must inevitably revert to their former state. To prevent this, it is imperative to constantly assemble slippery principles; to work out a system generating limitless distinctions.

Although a process of deconstruction is constantly underway, the problem is finding a concrete programme for including it within the structure of architectural production. One way would be to go outside the controlling framework of Modernist architecture, which forbids historical, regional and vernacular vocabulary, and to stitch together something which satisfies function solely by means of purely industrial methods. Several attempts have been made to rectify the situation by simply restoring the excluded vocabularies, but they have always been swallowed up by Modernism and have therefore done no more than simply expand the framework in which they were enclosed.

Following the crisis that I began experiencing in 1968, I resolved to initiate a thorough process of return to the compositional elements espoused by Modernism in its earliest phase. I decided to adhere to fundamental geometrical forms and to allow architectural configurations to emerge automatically from them. In this way I felt I would be able to suppress the aesthetic appreciation cultivated in me as a result of a Modernist background, while at the same time escaping from the patched functionalist compositional system. By means of a fundamental process of reduction, I intended to delve into the basis of the Modernist vocabulary, and by doing so, bring about its dissolution. This is the meaning of *maniera*, as explained earlier.

In the architectural forms evolved in this way, I made use of Euclidean geometric figures encapsulated in such Platonic solids as the cube and the cylinder. While experimenting with these forms, I encountered another great theoretical barrier.

As long as they are used in concepts of sketched plans, points, lines, surfaces and solid bodies they obey a certain consistent set of principles. However, when introduced into the concrete, social context of an actual architectural design, they take on the wider meanings of architectural vocabulary. In other words, vertical lines become posts or mullions and horizontal planes become ceilings and floors. In multi-dimensional compositions, the needs of their numbers determine their positions. In short, these figures are able to preserve their purely abstract geometrical natures only in the imagination. When used in architecture, which is fated to have a social mission, they are inevitably realised in ways that reflect a social vocabulary. Rejecting this kind of transformation into architectural vocabulary, Modernist design attempted to produce buildings that, in appearance, were sculpturesque or mechanical. Functionalists attempted to escape this connection altogether. However, the question ought to be not how to prevent but how to encourage such transformation to architecture.

From the time *maniera* was defined as an automatic stylistic movement, it depended on the characteristic, broader historical syntax of 'architecture'. It should be possible to abstract the stylistic nature of historical, regional and local items of architectural vocabulary just as readily as it is to abstract those from Modernist vocabulary. A kind of atavism born of manipulating pure forms led me to revert to the distinctive vocabulary of 'architecture'. Until that time I had wagered everything on the amplification of pure solid forms. Even the robots which I had designed were assemblies of cubes, spheres and cylinders. The Gunma Prefectural Art Museum was made up of an infinite assembly of cubes, as was the Kita-Kyushu Library of cylinders.

When the Fujimi Country Club was completed I became aware that the cut-cylinder section in its facade was a negative version of the entrance porch of Palladio's Villa Poiana. Suddenly, a building that was supposed to have been the outcome of the manipulation of pure geometric forms evoked an historical architectural example.

To discover the sources of this phenomenon, I analysed examples of classical style architecture and learned that without exception they all employed Platonic solid figures. Furthermore, I discovered that those eighteenth-century master architects with whom I had felt the greatest affinity since my student days, most vigorously exposed geometry in their exterior designs. Modern architects such as Le Corbusier are no exception.

Approaching classical compositional principles led to my criticism of Japanese Modern architecture. In Japan, traditional architecture had demonstrated virtually no concern with three-dimensional, solid spatial composition and had instead preferred to sever time into instances and space into floor areas, and to organise these fragments with intervals (*ma*) among them.

With this connection in mind, in 1978 I organised an exhibition called '*Ma*, Japanese Time–Space' for the Paris Festival d'Automne. This was an attempt to stimulate the introduction of more multi-dimensionally oriented spaces into a modern Japanese architecture that found itself, if subconsciously,

Arata Isozaki, The Museum of Modern Art, Gunma

unable to break from the tradition of assembling flat, floor-space-like areas.

Discovering the Platonic solid within classical compositional principles forced me to put myself outside the game. In other words, in order to get outside the Modernist architectural vocabulary, I once again had to articulate the Platonic solids within classical architectural vocabulary. Behind the assembly of classical architecture is the mega-vocabulary called 'Architecture' with a capital 'A'. All classical works of architecture and all contemporary architectural concepts whose inner and outer aspects can be discussed, started with that piece of mega-vocabulary called Architecture, and arrived at a definite form after a process of searching.

If Architecture with a capital 'A' is the text, then we must give thought to what was vigorously discussed all over the world in the seventies as 'intertextuality'. In the circumstances envisaged by this doctrine, the creative artist is, like Sisyphus, constrained to work limitless changes within the spaces of intertextuality. Thinking of this, I could not help recalling the transition from nothingness to creativity, the boundless progress, and the ideas of avant-garde leadership that the Modernists attempted to force upon us and the way all those ideas have collapsed. At present, instead of being a hero striving for Utopia, the creative artist has no recourse but a rhetorical stirring-up of already confused signs to regenerate meaning and non-meaning.

An interest in classical composition leads naturally to the method of quoting, whereby an element is transposed from its context in an old work of architecture and is thus made to generate a new genre of meaning. Works by Michelangelo, Palladio, Mies van der Rohe, Le Corbusier and so on become not mere references, but sources of direct quotations that, in new contexts, give birth to metaphors.

Even after stimulating the independent movement of the *maniera* system, I saw that I could not escape from the mega-vocabulary framework of Architecture with a capital 'A'. When this happened, in addition to pure geometrical figures, quotations become conspicuous in my work. I quoted systems, formerly complete in themselves, as metaphors functioning as references to generate different meanings.

I attempted to incorporate numerous metaphors in the works which I undertook in the latter half of the seventies. Though a decade ago, metaphor was of course my intention, the things that I used were intangible and conceptual: darkness, twilight, blankness and so on. Later they became more directly figurative and recognisable: water, hollow, question mark, binoculars, ship, carriage, cave, the plaza on the Capitoline Hill in Rome, Daphne, serrate columns and so on. The highly varied sources of the quotations ranged from actual historical works of architecture, to popular everyday articles, to items so small that interpretation of them was virtually impossible. My criterion for selection was the power to evoke metaphor.

As a consequence of this process of thought, my architectural work may seem to lack overall consistency. Although I have been repeatedly criticised for this, I consider it an important characteristic and even an inevitable element in my rebellion against Modernist architecture.

1980 STYLE IN RUINS:
TIME AND SPACE = TIME AND HISTORY

■ During the eighties I was in my fifties. Although I have said that I experience some kind of crisis every decade, during this period, with an architectural office to operate and a constant stream of work to do, I could not afford to take to my bed. Even without a severe crisis, I underwent a change in methodology that gave a new aspect to the *maniera* doctrine I propounded during the seventies.

In terms of political metaphor, throughout the sixties I advocated a guerrilla-like destructive operation, the major theme of which was criticism of Modernist architecture. Our generation came to be called the 'Dissolution Generation', from the title of one of my books, *Kenchiko no kaitai* (The Dissolution of Architecture).

The philosophy firmly formulated by Modernist architecture fused function and form, advocating a kind of Utopian progress, and gave rise to the so-called International Style, which was supposed to be universal. I, however, felt that all of this should be broken down and that reconstruction should begin from the point at which architectural discourse had been reduced to zero. My doctrine of *maniera*, influenced by Russian formalism, was an attempt to put the automatic movement of forms at the core of architectural method. My strategy was to isolate architectural discourse from politics and society with the idea that an apolitical stance would become political.

The theories formulated on the basis of the rectilinear, utopian idea of progress that constituted the underpinnings of Modernist architecture throughout the world look like the kind of dissolution I mentioned earlier. In fact, however, those theories represented contextualism in the wider sense. Each place has its own physical, daily life, and cultural context. Since they are often evaluated on the basis of the extent to which they suit the context, new buildings are supposed to harmonise with already existing patterns.

However, in my opinion, finding reliable urban contexts in Japan constitutes a major difficulty. I therefore believe that new buildings should stimulate the creation of new contexts in their surroundings. This is why my buildings assume either an aggressive or a defensive posture in relation to their settings. The same attitude pervades my architectural criticism.

In other words, my doctrine of *maniera* is anti-contextualist. From the outset, my buildings are expected to generate discord with their settings. Suddenly a town hall that looks like a spaceship seems to have floated down to settle in what had been a calm, peaceful town. One of my buildings suggests a great whale swirling about at the base of a traditional castle stone wall. Another looks like a huge grounded sailing vessel. These and my bright red wall cutting through a green pastoral setting are all alien elements which frequently throw their environments into confusion.

The *maniera* method achieves transformations because once the struggle with the location is over, direct confrontation with the broader culture behind it becomes possible. In 1978 I developed this theme in the exhibition 'Ma, Japanese Time–Space'. The concept of *ma*, or interval, for which we Japanese require no explanation, pervades our lives and our art in general, as well as our feelings, methods and artistic awareness. For the sake of people from the West I attempted to explain it according to Western logic as far as possible. Elements presented in the exhibition included painting, sculpture, music, dramatic performance, gardening, architecture, poetry and daily life, along with the Japanese language essential to it. An oblique line traversing these elements was drawn and explained by means of objects, sounds, actions and words. Oddly enough, during this process, the theories I had considered peculiarly Japanese dissolved as if some kind of solvent had been poured on them. In other words, when the Western world was superimposed on the Japanese, a gap was generated and deconstruction automatically occurred.

The Tsukuba Centre building, designed immediately after this 1978 Paris exhibition, represents my attempt to deconstruct Western elements by means of Japanese elements. Tsukuba was the sole new town project by the Japanese government after World War II. The Tsukuba Centre building is a complex facility at its core. In its design, I referred to a number of buildings from the classical tradition of the West. From the details in which these classical references were embodied, they eliminated all traces of a unifying system that might extend outwards to the whole. Consequently, the elements quoted from heterogeneous sources overlap in a fragmented and non-continuous way. I refer to this ironically as schizophrenic eclecticism. My approach in this instance can be said to resemble the way traditional Japanese architecture and garden designs evade totalising systems by employing non-compositional, non-hierarchical compositional principles. Looking back, I see that the Tsukuba Centre design is a mixture of classical precedents, Modernist elements and references to my own past works. In it, however, my most profound concern was devoted to the disjunctive placing of elements.

The Tsukuba Centre's central plaza is sunken. Deciding to use a sunken area was another step towards avoiding an overall totalising system. In addition, it implies political metaphor: by eliminating the element that should hint at its presence, I created a void at the heart of a place that should have been a stage for the Japanese nation. Whereas during the seventies I had appeared all the more political by refraining from political discussion, at this point I found myself in a position where connections with politics were forced upon me. I used irony to deal with this situation – eliminating the centre – though I only did so as a result of being placed in confrontation with the nation.

In the case of the design for the Museum of Contemporary Art in Los Angeles, I confronted political elements from the very outset. The city of Los Angeles is located at a point of confluence between the culture of the East and the West. Inevitably an oriental architect called to work there must provide a methodological interpretation of both cultures. To satisfy this demand, I refined my design approach into a homage to the golden section, as the Western method of establishing divisions, and the Yin and Yang philosophy, as the corresponding Eastern method.

From my experience superimposing the Western and the Japanese to generate gaps for interpretation and construction, I was able to design in an ambivalent way, to produce something that is neither oriental nor occidental while being both. During the process, I myself was drawn into a vortex of examination and interpretation arising from the collision of heterogeneous cultures.

The flow stimulated by the vortex resulting from the use of a central sunken patio and the galleries housed in two flanking wings apportioned on the basis of the golden section, has been treated similarly to the excursion path that plays an important role in many traditional Japanese-garden designs. This simultaneously realised both Eastern and Western spatial divisions.

The architectural forms projecting above ground are based on Platonic solids but at the same time allude to such historical precedents as the pyramids, Palladio, the palazzo, and so on. Juxtaposing the abstract and the concrete, the modern and the classical, and hard and smooth materials results in ambivalence. Nothing is clearly quoted as a reference source, nor did I intend to revive any single style. Instead, my aim was to dismantle apparently integrated architectural styles and to fragment them so that, at the moment when they seem to be in ruins, a

Arata Isozaki, Tsukuba Civic Centre, conceptual perspective

schizophrenic state of suspension is created. The fragments lose their birthplaces and points of origin. Dispersed as forms, shapes, elements and pieces devoid of meaning in the space called contemporary time, they flash on and off through the operation of metaphor. The effective method in this case is assembling fragments, as in a collage or a patchwork quilt.

It is necessary to point out that under such circumstances all architectural style is reduced to ruins. The only things available for architectural design are the fragments scattered about in the ruins. Should reconstruction be accomplished, the results would no doubt still resemble ruins. This is the reason why architecture must become schizophrenic and eclectic. The art of assembling fragments in a given place to intersect with the local context is political in nature. Consequently, architecture may well have to be reinterpreted on the basis of political significance. When this happens, architecture will find itself under a new programme of discourse.

ARCHITECTURE WITH OR WITHOUT IRONY

■ For the first twenty years of my career as a professional architect, I believed that architecture could only be accomplished by irony.
It was to make the very gap that would never be filled, a springboard.
It could combine even what was unreasonable.
It could allude to treason.
It made it possible to create architecture as criticism.
It could admire the vulgar against the noble, the secular against the sacred, without shame.
It could justify various vexations such as political estrangement, the handicaps of a foreigner, coming from a remote region, minor culture, bad conditions of economy, poor devices, non-orthodoxy, etc.

Ruins, doomsday, collapse and death were spoken about with nostalgia.
It was an unfulfilled wish, a mourning for what was lost – Hiroshima, holocaust.
To bridge the gap –
Wit, a sense of humour and paradox were adopted.
It was a limited measure allowing speech in an inorganic architectural language.
It could also save an architect from falling into a trap which would make him anonymous.
After twenty years of practical experience, I am now going to find a method of creating architecture without irony.
The architectural languages which I have adopted up to the present will be used continuously and some new ones will be developed.

However, ruins, regardless of the pathetic sentiment for what was lost, will remain as they are, according to the law of nature.
Doomsday, not as a fear of what is coming, will become the fact which can be seen.
Death will also be loved just like life.
Wit, to be as light as possible.
A sense of humour evokes what would vanish.
Paradox is used to make what is invisible, visible.
But, not cynically, not desperately.
To be dreaming of architecture as a pleasure machine.

Arata Isozaki, Donau-City Tower, Vienna, sketch